THE THEATRE GUILD

presents

BELLS ARE RINGING

A Musical Play

Book and Lyrics by

BETTY COMDEN and ADOLPH GREEN

Music by

JULE STYNE

Entire Production Directed by

JEROME ROBBINS

Sets and Costumes Designed by

RAOUL PENE DU BOIS

Orchestrations by

ROBERT RUSSELL BENNETT

Musical Director

MILTON ROSENSTOCK

Vocal Arrangements and Direction by HERBERT GREENE and BUSTER DAVIS

Lighting by PEGGY CLARK

Dance Arrangements and Incidental Scoring by JOHN MORRIS

Dances and Musical Numbers Staged by

JEROME ROBBINS and BOB FOSSE

Price $25.00

First Performance at the Shubert Theatre New York, Nov. 29, 1956

BELLS ARE RINGING

THE CAST

(In order of Appearance)

SUE	Jean Stapleton
GWYNNE	Pat Wilkes
ELLA PETERSON	Judy Holliday
CARL	Peter Gennaro
INSPECTOR BARNES	Dort Clark
FRANCIS	Jack Weston
SANDOR	Eddie Lawrence
JEFF MOSS	Sydney Chaplin
LARRY HASTINGS	George S. Irving
TELEPHONE MAN	Eddie Heim
LUDWIG SMILEY	Frank Milton
CHARLES BESSEMER	Frank Green
DR. KITCHELL	Bernie West
BLAKE BARTON	Frank Aletter
ANOTHER ACTOR	Frank Green
JOEY	Tom O'Steen
OLGA	Norma Doggett
MAN FROM CORVELLO MOB	John Perkins
OTHER MAN	Kasimir Kokich
CAROL	Ellen Ray
PAUL ARNOLD	Steve Roland
MICHELLE	Michelle Reiner
MASTER OF CEREMONIES	Eddie Heim
SINGER AT NIGHTCLUB	Frank Green
WAITER	Ed Thompson
MAITRE d'HOTEL	David McDaniel
POLICE OFFICER	Gordon Woodburn
MADAME GRIMALDI	Donna Sanders
MRS. MALLET	Jeannine Masterson

Dancers

Girls: Norma Doggett, Phyllis Dorne, Patti Karr, Barbara Newman, Nancy Perkins, Marsha Rivers, Beryl Towbin, Anne Wallace.

Boys: Doria Avila, Frank Derbas, Don Emmons, Eddie Heim, Kasimir Kokich, Tom O'Steen, Willy Sumner, Ben Vargas, Billy Wilson.

Singers

Girls: Pam Abbott, Joanne Birks, Urylee Leonardos, Jeannine Masterson, Michelle Reiner, Donna Sanders.

Boys: Frank Green, Marc Leon, David McDaniel, Paul Michael, Julian Patrick, Steve Roland, Ed Thompson, Gordon Woodburn.

7/63

Musical Program

ACT I

ACT II

Bells Are Ringing
Overture

JULE STYNE

Con brio
49
Vlns.
etc.
Saxs.
Trb.
Hrns.
p
cresc.
add 2nd & 3rd Tpts.
57
muted Tpt. solo
mf
Str.
1.
2.
74
Vlns. 8va
Hrns., Saxs.
82
unis. Br.
90

98
106
Str.
114
Tpt. Solo
In a slow two
8va
Vln.Cl.
mf
Br.
f-p
Vln.Cl. loco
mp
130
Fl.E.H.
Trb.
Hrns.
mf
etc.

138
Fl.Cl. E.H.
146
Vlns.
W.W.
Br.
154
Fl. E.H.
Trb. Solo
mf
Tutti
160
Gay waltz
mf

176
f
188
W. W., Str.
Beguine tempo
202
Hrn, Cello
206
f Tutti
Str.

etc.
214
Saxs., Str. 8va
Trb., Hrns.
Brass
Tutti
222
Saxs.
Str.
Hrns.
etc.

230
Saxs.
L.H.
rall.
Presto
Str., W. W.
Br.
f
Str., Cl., Pno.
Tutti
sfz
Attacca

No. 1

Opening
(Bells Are Ringing)

Lyrics by
BETTY COMDEN and
ADOLPH GREEN

Music by
JULE STYNE

mag - ine the sight, Me on the town in some be - witch - ing gown.
37
But I just wait at the end of the line, As bells are ring - ing, the
viennoise
bells keep ring - ing, Oh why, oh why, can't the next call be mine? ———
rit.
a tempo
49
ANNOUNCER: A sad story, girls - - - - But it need not have happened. - - - - Perhaps - - - during
Celeste
Strs.
p
the time you were out - - HE called, but no one was there to answer your telephone. - - - - - Don't let the same thing

* This Telephone Bell effect for Celeste and Triangle will occur wherever the music stops.

No. 2 It's A Perfect Relationship

Warning: JEFF: *(off stage) sings* "Taps."
Cue: Ella pulls plug.

17
can't see me. I'm in love with a voice: Pla - za oh, dou - ble four, dou - ble
three. What a per - fect re - la - tion - ship, I talk to him, and
Fl.
he just talks to me. And yet I can't help won - d'ring
Fl.
27
what does he look like?
Br.
mf
W.W. 8va
Br.
I wish I
Br.
W.W. 8va

35
knew. What
Br.
Br.
p
does he look like? Is he six foot sev - en or
39
pizz. Str.
Cl.
pp
three foot two? Has he eyes of brown or ba - by blue?
Big and might - y or un - der - fed? Trim black mus - tache or beard of red?
p
47
Can he dance like Fred As - taire? Is he dark or is he fair?
Br.
mp

Pom - pa - dour or not a hair? Well, I don't care! I'm in
mf Tutti
55
love with a man: Pla - za oh, dou - ble four, dou - ble three.
pizz. Str.
p
Hrn., Cello
W.W.
61
What a per - fect re - la - tion - ship! And that's how things should
al - ways be. Our love can nev - er lose its mys - ter - y, 'cause I'll
poco rit.
nev - er meet him, and he'll nev - er meet me,
Vlna.
pp a tempo
rall.

No, he'll nev - er meet me.
Cymb.
[In 4]
[In 2] (a tempo)
73
What does he look like,
Br.
Str.
f
p
My sleep - ing
prince?
What
Hrns.
does he look like?

He could be the fat and bald - ing type_ Or rug - ged tweeds and a
Fl.
p
Br.
89
bri - ar pipe,_ Dark-rimmed glass - es, sup - er mind,_
Br.
Br.
fp
Or the sweet po - et - ic kind,_ It does - n't mat - ter
Br.
fp
Telephone Buzzer
what he'd be_ How he'd love me!
mf
[Dance]—Cue: 4 boys shout Hooray!
Fast-In 3
ff

Str.
5
6
Hrns.
108
+W.W.
116
Str.
5
6
Hrns.
124
+W.W.
Hp.
Str., Tpt.
gliss.
132
Sax.
Hrns.
7

7
L.H.
7
Hrns.
144
Br.
Str., Hrns.
Wd. Blk.
152
Celesta
Pno., Br.
Celesta
160
+Str., Saxs.
+Tpts.
Trbs.

ELLA: I can just imagine what a date with him would be like.
Trb.
Hp.
Tutti
168
Moderato - In 4
Vla. 8va, Cello
Celesta
pp
Vlns.
Cls. (8 va)
Hns. (loco)
+ Cl.
+ Fl.

Tpts. 8va
Trbs. (loco)
Ob. Solo
Celesta
Vlns.
L.H.
Ob.
Vlns.
Hrns., Trb.
L.H.
Str. + Cym.
(Pno.)
ELLA: Mad, mad, mad, mad!
Br.
(laugh--kiss)
+W.W. 8va
Br.
etc.
Hp.
Telephone buzzer
Slowly
ELLA: (talks)
ELLA: Susanswerphone.
JEFF: Hello, Mom, if Olga calls again, stall her for me, will you?
ELLA: Yes, Mr. Moss.
JEFF: That's good old mom.
ELLA: Yes, Mr. Moss.
But he's
pp Celesta solo

100
Slower (In 4)
still just a voice; Pla - za oh, dou - ble four, dou - ble
pizz. Str.
pp
three.
Fl.
(Sings)
What a per - fect re - la - tion - ship, I
can't see him, he can't see me, He calls me "mom," he thinks I'm six - ty three, And I'll
(Celeste)
110
nev - er meet him and he'll nev - er meet me,
Vln. A
a tempo
rall.
Bright tempo
No, he'll nev - er meet me.
She sits down.
cresc.
dialogue

No. 3

Mambo Montage

Cue: SUE: They don't care about you.

No. 4 Independent

Cue: JEFF: ---I've learned the great lesson of independence.

Now I'm liv - in', I'm on my own. Go-ing it a-lone.
fz
21
I don't need an - y - one And no one needs me.
No need for an - y - one to help me mix mar - ti - nis, roast the wee - nies,
fz
p W.W.
bake the bli - nies, now that I'm free. Self - suf - fi - cient, self - sup - port - ing.
31
Tutti
p
muted Br.
Trav - 'ling light and fly - ing so - lo; Ev - 'ry day is In - de - pen - dence

37
ALL: Hoo-ray!
day, Hoo-ray! Free and eas-y, Blithe and breez-y,
Br.
sf
W.W.
Go-ing it a - lone; I'm in-de-pen-dent and on my
Br cut off.
W.W.
45
Faster-Dance tempo
own.
Str.
p
cresc.
f add Trbs.
muted Tpts.
49
+W.W. 8va
Trbs. & Hrns.

61
Br. flutter
Trbs.
Hrns.
W.W. Str. etc.
fzp
W.W.
pizz. Str.
71
sfz
79
(vaudeville bit)
(JEFF does lion tamer bit with a chair)
Saxs.
Br.

87
GROUP:
JEFF:
GROUP:
In - de - pen - dent!
In - de - pen - dent!
Self - suf - fi - cient!
Rhythm
etc.
JEFF:
add GROUP:
Self-suf-fi-cient! Ev - 'ry day is
In - de-pen-dence day,
Hoo-ray!
Sax.+Str.
fp
95
Free and eas - y,
Blithe and breez-y,
Go-ing it a -
lone.
In - de - pen - dent,
self - suf - fi - cient,
on his
cresc.
own
Hoo - ray!
gliss.
(House phone buzzes)
sffz

No. 5 You've Got To Do It

Cue: JEFF: Ma, you're right and I will! Seven o'clock.

At cue:
16
wonder how I would look with a mustache--etc.
--hurt my tennis game --- etc.
--little drinko! --- etc.
You play quite well for a loser. Really, you play very --
The play!
Vlns., Harp
p
on Cue:
Timp.
Tria. solo
21
Vivo
25
You've got to do it!
Str. + W.W.
etc.
Br. cut off.
You've got to do it! Got to do it all a - lone. No-one else - 'll do it
(Spoken)
All right, start some place else. etc.
for you, Bud - dy boy! — You're on your own. —
Br.
sf

36
At cue:
--Wouldn't it be terrible if I froze in this position? etc.
---get in shape when the play's on.
The play!
Vlns., Harp
on Cue:
Timp.
Tria.
41
Vivo
45
You've got to do it!
mf Br. cut off
You've got to do it! Got to do it all a - lone. No-one else-'ll do it
Ah, what's the use, I'll never make it alone.
for you, Bud - dy boy!
Br.
mf
add Timp.
f
Lights fade and traveller closes.
55
Presto
ff
sffz
attacca
Timp.

No. 6 It's A Simple Little System

SHANDOR:
19
Slowly
Fl.,Cl.
It's a simple little system any child can understand; The composers' names, we list 'em — with the race-tracks of the land. With this
p Str.
(+ Harp.)
Ob.
simple little system, we'll be close by fortune's door.. And to think that no one ever, ever
Bssn.
thought of it before.
(Ha-ha) Gentlemen, look at your charts!
What is
Cl.
p Str.
p Str.
29
MAN:
SHANDOR:
2nd MAN:
SHANDOR:
Beethoven? Belmont Park.
Where's Puccini? Pimlico.
Who is
+W.W.
tr
3

35
Allegretto
3rd MAN:
Hum-per-dinck? Hol-ly-wood.
SHANDOR:
What is Bee-tho-ven?
poco rall.
p poco a poco cresc.
Str. unis
ALL:
Bee-tho-ven is Bel-mont Park.
SHANDOR:
Where is Puc-ci-ni?
ALL:
Puc-ci-ni is Pim-li-co.
+Tpts.
+Trbs.
SHANDOR:
Who is Hum-per-dinck?
ALL:
Hum-per-dinck is Hol-ly-wood.
47
Moderato
SHANDOR:
That is cor-rect. Turn the page. What's Tchai-kow-sky?
(Solo)
MAN:
Church-ill Downs.
SHANDOR:
Who's Mous-sorg-sky?
(Solo)
MAN:
Mon-mouth Park.
SHANDOR:
What's Rach-man-in-off?
GIRL: (Raucously)
Rock-ing-ham.
p Str.+W.W.
+W.W.
tr

55 Allegretto
SHANDOR: What's Tchai - kow - sky?
ALL: Tchai - kow - sky is Church - ill Downs.
SHANDOR: Who's Mous - sorg - sky?
ALL: Mous - sorg - sky is Mon - month Park.
SHANDOR: What's Rach - man - in - off?
ALL: Rach - man - in - off is Rock - ing - ham.
SHANDOR: That is cor - rect. Turn the page.
ALL: It's a
69
sim - ple lit - tle sys - tem, we're im - pa - tient to be - gin,
GIRLS: Oh yes, oh yes.
Sim - ple lit - tle sys - tem,
ALL: when the law is list - 'ning in.
SHANDOR: (Sings) We will
W.W. + Hrns.
Str. unis
p
+Tpts.
+Trbs.
add 8va Vlns. & Fl.
Hrns., Vlas.

(Sings)
take those record orders in a very cultured tone, While we're
p
really booking horses over at Sus-ans-wer-phone. We'll be
ALL:
Tempo a piacere
mf
f
rich! We'll be rich! We'll be rich!
p
mf
f
81
Allegretto
De-bus-sy is Del-mar, Hum-per-dinck is Hol-ly-wood.
W.W.
mf
Ce-sar Franck is Fair-Grounds, Si-bel-i-us is Sports-man's park.
etc.

89
Ber - li - oz is Bain - bridge, Hin - de - mith is Haw - thorne.
SHANDOR: Ev'rybody, all together, now!
MEN:
ff
Of - fen - bach is O - ma - ha...
Who is
Tutti
rall.
96 Grandioso
GIRLS:
It's a sim - ple lit - tle sys - tem.
TENORS:
ff
Bee - tho - ven? Bel - mont Park.
Who's Puc - ci - ni? Pim - li -
BARITONES BASSES:
ff
Bee - tho - ven? Bel - mont Park.
Who's Puc - ci - ni? Pim - li -
Str.
etc.
ff

Sim- ple lit- tle sys- tem.
Ken- tuck- y. _ And Shos- ta - ko- vich is
co.
Who's Tchai - kow- sky? Church- ill Downs.
And Shos- ta - ko- vich is
co.
Who's Tchai - kow- sky? Church- ill Downs.
And Shos- ta - ko- vich is
104
Tempo Pomposo
SHANDOR:
What is Han- del?
Sar- a- to- ga!
Hi- a - le - ah, Hi- a - le - ah.
Sar- a- to- ga!
Hi- a - le - ah, Hi- a - le - ah.
Sar- a- to- ga!
Hi- a - le - ah, Hi- a - le - ah.

Who is Han-del?
Hi-a-le-ah, Hi-a-le-ah. Oh, what a
Hi-a-le-ah, Hi-a-le-ah. Oh, what a
Hi-a-le-ah, Hi-a-le-ah. Oh, what a
sys-tem.
sys-tem.
sys-tem.
sf
attacca

No. 6 A Change Of Scene

No. 7 Change Of Scene

Cue: ELLA: I mean, Max's dog and cat house!

(Blackout)

No. 8 Is It A Crime?

Cue: ELLA: Sometimes I can't tell right from wrong. I wish you'd help me.

13
Tempo a piacere
Is it a crime to start each day with a laugh and a smile and a song? And
p
Str.
is it a crime to end each day with a laugh and a smile and a song? Is it wrong? Is it a
21
crime to call the world your val - en - tine? Is it a
Cello
crime to grab a lamp post And then sing Sweet Ad-o - line, I ask you?
29
Is it a crime to save a wee ba - by bird when it falls from its nest?
a tempo
Harp

That lit - tle bird should have a chance to fly like all the rest.
Celeste
37
Faster
If it's a crime to help old la - dies cross the street, Then
add Br. W.W.
Slower (In four)
put me in jail! With - out bail! Bread and wa - ter from an old tin pail, If
(Optional)
that, if that's a crime.
Fl. 8va
a tempo
Solo Vln.
Str. only
49
Freely
She stops singing and talks---
Inspector Barnes, I'm puzzled. We're taught two things as we go through life: One: Be
Is it a crime - - -
Str. Quartette
pp

Sung:
Spoken:
thy brother's keeper and Two: Mind your own business.
Now, if I know
With a laugh and a smile and a song.
a tempo
57
something --- and by telling it to some-one in distress, I could change that some-one's life and
faster
64
Slower
bring him ---
Sung:
Slow (In four)
[In two]
Spoken: Is it a crime to tell him? Or is it
The blue bird of hap - pi - ness.
rit. as necessary
colla voce
a tempo
a crime not to? Is it "you must-n't," or "you've got to"?
Should you say, "Hey, watch out for that banana peel, Bud" Or
just remain silent - - - - - - - - then laugh as he
rit. as necessary
Sung:
Spoken:
Inspector Barnes, my job is to get messages to people on time.
crash - es with a thud!
Harp
Vlns.
Slowly (In two)
gliss.

74
With music:
If I have a job, and I see it through, And it's just my du-ty that I
mf Tutti
Slower (In four)
Spoken:
Inspector, let's
do, do, do, Is that, is that----
3
3
80
go back a few thousand years. If there had been answering services then–And it had been up to me, I could have prevented many
Solo Vln.
Str. only
a famous tragedy. I could have changed the course of history----
Fast (In two)
Sung:
Spoken: Why,
With a laugh and a smile and a song----
rit. as necessary
a tempo
88
every night I lie in bed and my cheeks get soaking wet when I think what I could have

* Orchestra crescendos at the words "I'm telling you."

No. 8A Change Of Scene

No. 9

Better Than A Dream

Cue: JEFF: ... outline

Moderately - In 2

41
bet - ter, bet - ter than a dream. What is real
W.W.
Cello
is more i - deal than a dream. To see and hear you, To
49
Br.
be so near you is bet - ter, bet - ter than a dream.
+ Trbs.
57
mp
mf
65
JEFF:
Can this be a dream? Can I still be a - sleep on the couch there?
W.W.
p
Cello

73
Can this girl be real - ly here? She seems to know by
sheer in - tu - i - tion How I land-ed in this con-di - tion. Boy, does she know me -- And the
way that I think, The way that I drink, The fact that I slept all year. _
Br.
83
But it's not a dream 'Cause, look, I've got some
W.W.
Cello
Rhythm
etc.
words on the pa - per. Stead - y, boy, _ don't faint or

91
scream, Don't ask who sent you this an - gel_ _ It's bet - ter, bet - ter than a dream.
ELLA:
You're
+Hn.
ff
99
bet - ter, bet - ter than a dream.
JEFF:
Can this be a dream? Can I still be a - sleep on the couch there?
p
What you are is bet - ter far than a dream. I
Can this girl be real - ly here? She

107
tried to pic - ture your face, But
seems to know by sheer in - tu - i - tion How I land - ed in this con - di - tion.
now I see you, You're out of this world, You're out of this sphere, You're
Boy, does she know me -- And the way that I think, The way that I drink, The
117
out of that out - er space.
You're bet - ter, bet - ter than a
fact that I slept all year.
But it's not a dream 'cause,
dream.
What is real is more i - deal than a dream.
look, I've got some words on the pa - per. Stead - y, boy, don't faint or scream.

No. 9 A

Telephone Incidental

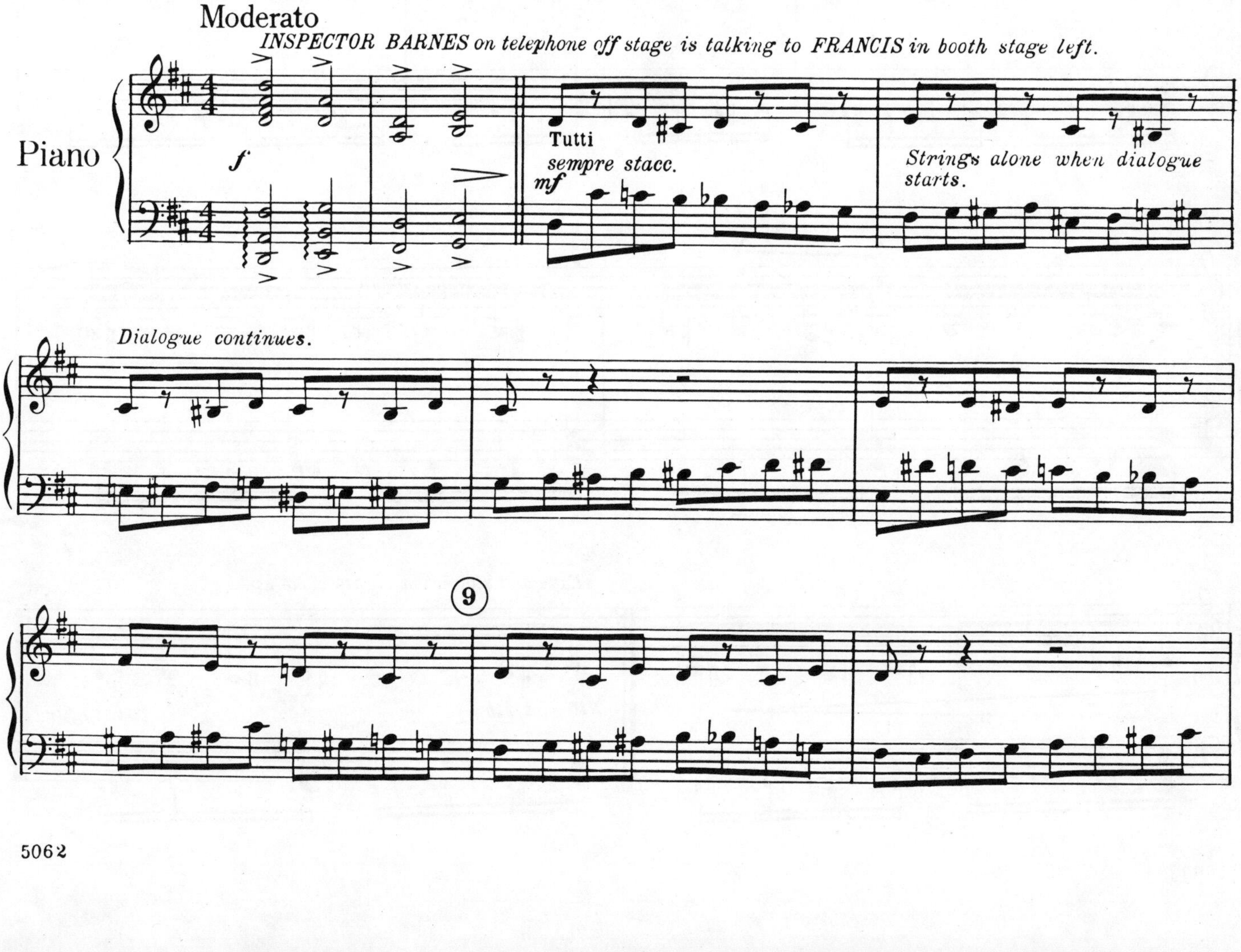

No. 9B Change Of Scene To Subway

No. 10 Hello, Hello There

Cue: 3rd MAN shakes hands.

*Hold this measure until everyone has shaken hands.

It's a pleas-ure and a priv'-lege! Glad to know you! How are you? Hel-lo!
Cls.
30
MAN: (Spoken)
Let's have a par-ty and pour out the wine!
ALL: Yeah!
2nd MAN: (Spoken)
I've got sa-la-mi!
3rd MAN (Spoken)
So ev'-ry-thing's fine!
Fl.,Vln.
pizz.
Vla.,Cello
38
ALL: (Sung)
Let's sing to-geth-er and let out a yell.
'Sal-ways fair weath-er when we're sing-ing---
Subway stops. More people get on and are greeted by the passengers.
47
ALL:
Hel-lo, hel-lo there!
Fl.,Cl.
Str.
Br.,Hrns.
Pleased to meet you! It's a pleas-ure
W.W.
Hrns.
Trbs.

and a priv'-lege! Glad to know you___ How are you? Hel - lo!
Harp gliss.
59
GIRLS:
MEN: Hel-lo, hel - lo, hel - lo, hel -
Hel - lo, hel - lo there, ___ Pleased to meet you!
Vln.
etc.
Br.
lo there, hel - lo, hel - lo, hel - lo, hel - lo, hel - lo, hel - lo.
It's a pleas - ure and a priv-lege! Glad to know you! How are you? Hel - lo!
Harp gliss.
71 Polka
ALL
Well, well, what do you know? We should have
Fl.,Cl.
etc.
Str., Hrns.
mf
Bssn.
79
done this a long time a - go! Well, well, is - n't it
Fl.Cl.
etc.
Str.

85
swell! Is - n't it nice to say: Hel - lo, hel - lo there!
p Hrns., Cello
Pleased to meet you! How are you? Hel - lo!
Tutti
93
Subway stops again --- Sour man gets on ---
f
Br.
Harp gliss.
106
ALL
(Singing dies out)
Hel - lo, hel - lo there! pleased to meet you... It's a pleas-ure and a priv....
Str., Hrns.
Br.
Str. only

114
W.W., pizz. Str.
dim.
122
Br., W.W.
(Str. as before)
Str. only
130
ALL: Hello!
Br. W.W.
138
W.W. Str.
Tpts.
Trbs., Basses, Hrns.
146

158
GROUP ON STAGE: (With hands, etc.)
pizz. Str., WW
mf
Tpts.
cresc.
Tutti f
Harp
gliss.
168
Vlns. unis.
etc.
W.W.
Tpts.
Trbs., Cello
Vlns. (detaché)
(Tpts., W.W. as before)
Bass
Subway stops. All fall to floor.
Tpts. W.W.
180
ALL:
Well, well, what do you know! We should have done this a
1st Tpt., Trb., Fl.
mf pizz. Str.
188
long time a - go. Well, well, is - n't it swell----

194
Hel - lo, hel - lo there! Pleased to
Str.,Picc.
Tutti
f
Br.
mf
meet you! It's a pleas-ure and a priv'lege. Glad to know you. How are you? Hel - lo!
etc.
Allegro vivace
208
1st VOICE: Hello!
2nd: How are you?
3rd: Pleased to meet you!
4th: It's a pleasure!
W.W.
pizz. Str.
5th: It's a privilege.
6th: Glad to know you.
7th: Delighted!
8th: Charmed!
9th: Enchanted!
10th: Hello there!
p
11th: How's the family?
12th: Just fine!
13th: Bon jour!
14th: Hello!
222
Faster
Piano & Cls.
R.H.
mf
f
L.H.

Boy enters
sits down and reads newspaper.
232
People run across stage with whistles, cap guns etc.
W.W.
mf pizz. Str.
Picc., Cl., 1st Vlns.
f
Tpts. 2nd Vlns.
Trbs., Vla., Cello
242
W.W.
mf pizz. Str.
Picc., Cl., 1st Vlns.
Tpts., 2nd Vlns.
Trbs., Vla., Cello
8va
254
Str. Picc.
etc.
Tpt. 8va
Trbs., Bass, Cello

262
270
Acrobats enter.
Piano & Cls.
R.H.
f
L.H.
278
Picc., Cl., 1st Vlns.
f
Tpts., 2nd Vlns.
Trbs., Vla., Cello
286
Piano, W.W., 1st Vlns.
R.H.
Tpts., Vla.
L.H.
Trbs.
Bass
etc.
294
Picc., Cl., 1st Vlns.
f
Tpts., 2nd Vlns.
Trbs., Vla., Cello
Hrns
ff
Blackout.
(Ella is lifted on chair in the dark.)
Drum Solo

No. 10 A Change Of Scene

No. 11 I Met A Girl

Cue: ELLA: I'll come to your place next Wednesday --- six o'clock.
JEFF: Promise?
ELLA: Promise.

yet I guess she's real-ly rath-er spe-cial for a girl. For once you have seen her, the
oth-ers are out.
Hey! What am I get-ting so ex-cit-ed a-bout?
Cls.
mf Tutti
36
But so what, what has she got oth-ers have
Vlns.
W.W.
Str.
not?
Two eyes, two lips, a nose most
Hp., W.W.
44
girls have some of those.
Yet when
add Tpts & Hrns.
Vlns.
W.W.
Str.
52

she looks_ up at me, what_ do I see?_ The
60
most en - chant - ing face._ My pulse be - gins to
68
race. Hey! I met a girl,_ a mar-vel-ous girl!_ She's rar-er than u-
W.W.
Fl., Cl. 8va bassa
Tutti
(Hp. & Guitar as before)
Cls.
p
76
ran-i-um and fair-er than a pearl. I found me a trea-sure and I want to shout!_
84
Fl., Vlns.
This is what I'm get-ting so ex-cit-ed a-bout!_ I met a girl_ and
Str. W.W.
add Brass
Tutti

Faster
92
1st GROUP:
I fell in love — to - day. ———
He met a girl, —
W.W. 8va
f
Trbs., Cello
mf Str.
2nd GROUP:
3rd GROUP:
ALL:
100
He met a girl, —
He met a girl, —
A won-der-ful girl —
A mar-vel-ous girl —
add Brass
— A fab - u - lous girl —
A su-per sen - sa-tion-al girl!
Hp. gliss.
f
108
He met a girl, —
a won - der - ful girl, —
She's real - ly got a
Br., pizz. Str.
p no W.W.
116
lot to re-com-mend her for a girl.
A fab - u-lous crea - ture with - out an - y doubt.
Hrn.
mf Br. & Str.

JEFF:
This is what I'm get-ting so ex-cit-ed a-bout.
ALL:
No
Tpt.,Vln.
+Saxs.
Br. (optional)
+Str
124
ev-'ry day girl, A won-der-ful girl, A real-ly mar-vel-ous girl.
Saxs.
An ut-ter-ly fab-u-lous crea-ture with-out an-y doubt.
3
132
JEFF:
ALL:
This is what he's ex-cit-ed a-bout.
f
JEFF:
But so what? What has she got
Saxs.+Str.
subito p

148
ALL: div.
oth - ers have not? Two eyes, lips,
Br.
Str. & Saxs.
p
cresc.
nose, all girls have those.
156
JEFF:
Yet when she looks up at me, What does he see?
ALL:
Saxs.
pp
add Br.
MEN:
164
The most en - chant - ing face.
ALL:
His
Br
Str.
p Saxs.
Hrn.
(May be spoken - - - - - - - - - - - - - - - - - - -)
heart keeps beat - ing fast - er and fast - er and fast - er it goes. Hey!
Br. Str.
Saxs.
cresc.
Br.
Hp gliss.

174
JEFF:
I met a girl, a mar-vel-ous girl.
ALL:
She's rar-er than u-ran-i-um and fair-er than a pearl.
Tutti
JEFF: 182
I found me a trea-sure and I want to shout.
Saxs.
p
Br.
f
ALL:
This is what he's get-ting so ex-cit-ed a-bout
190 Du
He met a girl, such a
mf
ooo
won-der-ful girl.
Saxs.
He met a girl and he fell in love to-day.
(No Strings or Bass)
ff
He met a girl!
Lights fade
attacca

No. 11A Change Of Scene

No. 12 Change Of Scene

Cue: KITCHELL sings: "Oh, Mississippi steamboat around the bend --- Whooo! Whooo! ---

No. 12 A Drugstore Incidental

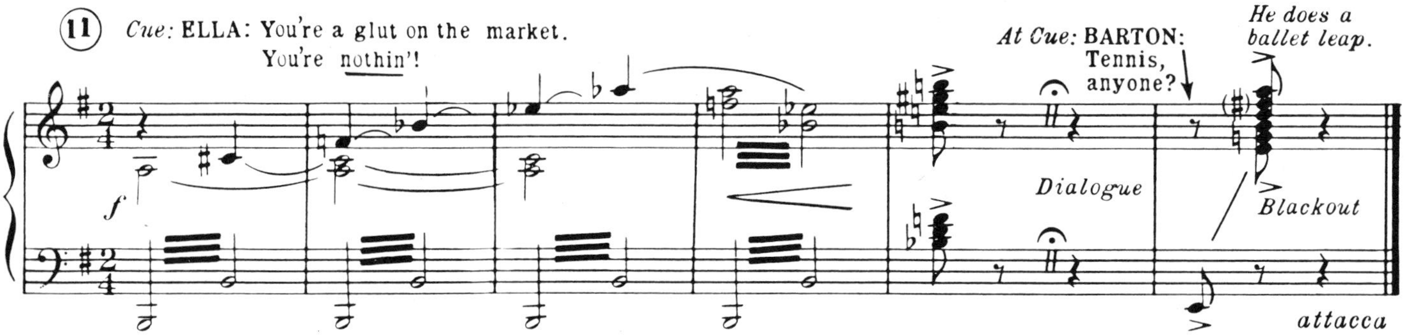

No. 12 B

Change Of Scene

No.12C Change Of Scene

Cue: ELLA screams and dashes out.

No. 13 Long Before I Knew You

Cue: **JEFF:** Where were we?
Act 12, Scene 9.

24
Long be-fore I knew you, Long be-fore I met you,
Hp.
mp Str.
E.H.
I was sure I'd find you Some day, some - how.
32
I pic-tured some-one who'd walk and talk and smile as you do, Who'd
Str.
make me feel as you do right now. All that was
Hrns.
Cello
40
long be-fore I held you, Long be-fore I kissed you,
E.H. 8va.
B.Cl.

48
Long be-fore I touched you and felt this glow.
But now you
Str.
real - ly are here and now at last I know
That long be-fore I knew you, I loved you
p
54
so.
Vln. espr.
pp
Str
ELLA:
Is that all?
JEFF:
But you didn't write anything down.
ELLA:
I didn't have to.
Cl., Vla.
59
She sings:
Long be-fore I knew you,
Long be-fore I met you,
Str.
p a little more rhythmic
W.W.
Fl. 8va
E.H.
Fl.
I was sure I'd find you, Some day, some - how.
Cello, Cl.

67
Vlns.
I pic - tured some - one who'd walk and talk and smile as you do, Who'd
Fl.
make me feel as you do right now.
ELLA: I really have
pp Str.
75
to go! JEFF: Mel, you can't! etc.... can't throw me back to the sharks. Mel, I love you!
+W.W.
Harp
Celeste
79
At Cue: The door opens and ELLA re-enters.
ELLA:
If it's a crime to help old la - dies cross the street - - -
Tutti
sf - p
Harp gliss.
Allargando
ff Tutti
Trb.
Curtain
End of Act I

Entr'acte

Brightly (In 3)
W.W.
Str.
Piano
ff
Trb.
2nd Trb. & Bass 8va bassa
poco allargando
13
molto espr.
Picc., Cl.
f Tutti
21
Tpts.
(Thumb melody)
Str.
Trb.
Picc., Cl., Vla.
29
Str., Br.
Harp, W.W., Saxs.
(Bass)

W.W.
37
8va
rall.
e dim.
43
Bright tempo
47
unis. Tpts.
f
55
63

71
79
87
Trb. Solo
Trbs.
W.W.
W.W.
3
95
103
Trbs.
111
unis. Tpts.
Hp. gliss.

119
131
sempre f
mf
139
Moderately (in four)
muted Tpt. Solo
147

155
Tutti
163
cresc., rit.
a tempo
rall.
173
p
Tutti
Hold until curtain starts up.
Str.
Br.
fz
8va
Gliss as ELLA clicks key.
gliss.

No. 14 Perfect Relationship (Waltz)

Warning: *SUE exits.*
Cue: GWYNNE: What's your excuse for seeing him tonight?
ELLA: Woman overboard!

49
57
65
73
77
85
89
97
Stop at Cue: CARL: You're dead if you can't Cha-Cha! Free lesson!
Then proceed directly to #15 "Mu-Cha-Cha."
(Optional repeat until Cue)

No. 15 Mu-Cha-Cha

at Cue:
"Here's Carl."
Str.
Fl.
W.W. only
p Repeat ad lib.
Cello
Str. W.W.
Optional number of bars
CARL: (When ready)
Aye, yi-yi, yi-yi.
Repeat ad lib.
ELLA:
Aye, yi-yi, yi-yi.
20
CARL: (Sung)
Mu-cha-cha, tell me do
W.W. 8va
p Str.
you cha-cha?
ELLA:
Me cha-cha? Señ-or, si si cha-cha.
Cls., Str.

GROUP: (Claps)
CARL:
Now, cha-cha, Please show me how cha-cha.
W.W. 8va
Str.
Cls., Str.
ELLA:
I got-cha, you watch-a cha-cha.
Str. only
+Br.
Str. only
+Br.
Tutti
ff Str. only
28
CARL:
Hey, cha-cha, is this the way, cha-cha?
Vlns.
etc.
Trbs.
ELLA:
Si, cha-cha, a-way we go cha-cha.

CARL:
Ay, cha-cha, I'm feel-ing high, cha-cha.
ALL:
Oh, such a hot-cha-cha, cha-cha.
Vlns.
etc.
Trbs.
36
(Clap)
ELLA:
Come a lit - tle clos-er, then a lit - tle clos-er,
Fls.
Cl. simile
Then you turn and walk a - way.
Ay, yi!
ALL:
Ta ta
Fls.
Vlns.
Cl., B.Cl. etc.
tum ta ta ta ta ta ti - ga, ti - ga, tum ta ta ta ta ta ti - ga, ti - ga,
Br.
Br.

Tum ta ta ta ta ta ti-ga, ti-ga, Tum ta ta ta ta ta ti-ga, ti-ga,
L.H.
CARL:
Come a lit - tle clos - er, then a lit - tle clos - er.
47
Don't go way_ my lit-tle Mu-cha-cha, the dance is through, cha-cha.
Str., W.W.
R.H.
ELLA:
Now, cha-cha, let's have some chow, cha-cha.
CARL:
Then, cha-cha, we'll dance a -
Str., W.W.
53
BOTH:
gain, cha-cha, Clos - er and clos - er and clos - er and clos - er and
R.H.

clos - er and clos - er to you,
Fl.
ELLA:
GROUP:
Mu-cha-cha!
58
ALL:
Mu-cha-cha.
Cha-cha-cha,
cha - cha-cha,
W.W., Str.
8va
One muted Tpt.
mf
Hrns.
Cha-cha-cha,
cha - cha-cha,
Cha - cha - cha,
8va
cha - cha-cha,
cha-cha!
8va
W.W., Vlns.

66
Ta ta tum ta ta ta ti - ga, ti - ga, Tum ta ta ta ta ta ti - ga, ti - ga,
mf muted Br.
Tum ta ta ta ta ta ti - ga, ti - ga, Tum ta ta ta ta ta ti - ga, ti - ga,
Hey! Hey! Hey! Hey! cha-cha!
W.W.,Hp.
mf Tutti
muffled Dr. Solo
poco a poco cresc.
etc.
75
ff Tutti
CAROL: Hey Carl, take me to the Pyramid Club! Me!
CARL:
Aye, yi - yi, yi - yi!
Vamp
p
pp

*Cluck-with the tongue.

si cha-cha.
Now, cha-cha, please show me how cha-cha.
98
I got-cha, you watch-a cha-cha.
Si, cha-cha, a-way we
W.W., Vlns.
Harp
Tutti
go cha-cha.
Hey, cha-cha, is this the way, cha-cha?
Trbs., Hrns.
Ay, cha-cha; I'm feel-ing high cha-cha.
Oh such a hot-cha-cha

(Clap)
106
Cha - cha!
8va W.W.
Str.
8va
Stomp-stomp stomp, Hey!
(Clap)
8va
8va
loco
ff Tutti
114
Dr. Solo
etc.
(Dr. Solo)
(Dr. Solo)

(Dr. Solo)
(Dr. Solo)
mf
120
8va
Hrns., 1st Trb.
8va
Br., W.W.
(Loco) add Tpts.
128
Drum Solo
132
Tutti
Trbs., Hrns

CHORUS: Hey!
R.H.
Tutti
Trbs., Hrns
R.H.
140
(Dancers shout, yell etc. ad lib. throughout drum solo)
Drum Solo (Augmented by three or four members of the orchestra playing gourds, claves, maraccas etc.)
muffled Sn.Dr.
Rim
S.D.
Cow bell
Rim
Cow bell
Rim
Cow bell
Rim
Cow bell
Rim
Cow bell
149
Rim
Tom Tom
Sn. Dr.
Cow bell
Rim
T.T.
Sn.Dr. muffled
T.T.
Sn. Dr.
C.B.
155
Sn.Dr.(muffled)
Rim, Tom Tom
Sn.Dr. muffled

161
Hi hat Cymb.
Temple Bl.
T.T.
Sn.Dr.(muffled)
Dr.
cresc.
poco
a
poco
pp
Br.
rip.
166
f
fz
fz
172
Br. rip up
(rip)
Tutti
Saxs
Saxs
(rip)
Saxs., Str.
Tutti
Repeat 5 times
Hey!
gliss.
gliss.
Cymb.
ff
attacca

No.15 A

Change Of Scene

*JEFF sings "Hello, hello there," as man passes him.

No. 16 Just In Time

Warning: ELLA: In the park?
JEFF: What's the matter? No guts?
Cue: He starts dancing her across the stage.

all were crossed, No where to go.
Br.
Fl.
19
Now you're here And now I know just where I'm go-ing; No more
Str.
p
Cls.
doubt or fear, I've found my way. For love came
Str. 8va
Br.
Cls.
Br.
27
just in time, You found me just in time,
Cls.
Br.
And changed my lone-ly life that love-ly day.
Tpt.
p

*After cue: "Let's slaughter em!" Vamp is played once more before proceeding to bar 39.

W.W., Str. pizz.
61
p subito
pp
ELLA : Hey!
W.W.
Br.
65
ff
fff
Str., Rhythm
JEFF: Hey, wait a minute! Don't give them everything.
pp
Str. pizz.
Br.
p
75
(Dumb chorus girl sound)
ELLA: (In a high nasal voice) (do de do do do de do)
(do de
JEFF: Just in time,
You found me just in time.
GROUP:
Hum
hum
Br. muted
pp

do de do de do de)
Do do.
This
Be-fore you came my time was run-ning
hum
act could play the Pal-la-di-um, or e-ven the Yan-kee Sta-di-um!
83
(He was
I was lost.
Hum
lost)
(They were tossed.)
(They were crossed.)
The los-ing dice were tossed.
My brid-ges all were crossed,
No where to
hum
hum

91
JEFF:
go.
GIRLS:
Oh, my dar - ling, Now you're here, And now I
BOYS:
Oh, my dar - ling, Now you're here, And now I
W.W.
Str. 8va
W.W.
Br.
W.W.
know just where I'm go - ing, Nev - er a doubt or fear, Now I'm on my
know just where I'm go - ing, Nev - er a doubt or fear, Now I'm on my
add Str.
add Br.
W.W., Hrns.
99 Slowly
JEFF:
For love came just in time, You found me
way.
ELLA: (In natural voice)
In time,
way.
Str.
Harp gliss.
p
dolce

Just in time, And changed my lone - ly life that love - ly
Just in time, And changed my lone - ly life that love - ly
day.
day.
GIRLS:
pp
Du ru du du, du ru du ru, Just in time, Du ru du du, du ru du ru, Just in time,
BOYS:
pp
Du ru du du, du ru du ru, Just in time, Du ru du du, du ru du ru, Just in time,
Fl.,Cl.
pp
f
Just in time.
f
Just in time.
Str., W.W.
L.H.
f
Tutti
attacca

No. 16 A Party Scene Incidental

33
41
At cue: MAN: Mary Pickford and Ethel Barrymore, segue as one to
"Drop That Name." # 17
1.
2.

No. 17 Drop That Name

Lou - ie Schurr and Court - ney Burr And Irv - ing La - zar, — An - tho - ny
Cl., Vla., Cello
ELLA:
Quinn, And Rin Tin Tin! —
W.W.
f Br.
14
GROUP:
Dor - is Day and Bar - ry Gray and
Str. (smoothly)
p
Ed - na Best, Ar - thur Loew and Vaughn Mon - roe, Re - bec - ca West,
Cl., Bsn.
Ir - win Shaw and Ev - e - lyn Waugh and Er - rol Flynn, Ror - y Cal - houn
ELLA:
And Rin Tin
Toon!
22
Bar - ney Ba - ruch and King Fa - rouk, Al - i - stair Cooke and Deb - bie and Ed - die,
W.W.
f
Br.
p Quasi legato
Vla., Cello
Vlns.
etc.

Lu-cille Ball and Laur-en Ba-call, Hed-y La-marr, Roz Rus-sell and Fred-die,
Car-ol Reed and Sam-my Snead and De-bor-ah Kerr,— An-na May
Cl.
Vla
Cello
ELLA: (Spoken)
Wong, And Rong, Tong, Tong!
ALL:
Ha-ha-ha, ha-ha-ha, ha-ha-ha, ha-ha-ha,
Tutti
f
Ha-ha-ha!—
Rim shot
Ha-ha-ha, ha-ha-ha, ha-ha-ha, ha-ha-ha, Ha-ha-ha!—
Rim shot
34
FELLOW: (Spoken)
Lunch-eon was fun at Twen-ty One, Then I had to run for drinks at the Pla-za.
W.W.
Quasi legato
Vla., Cello
Vlns.
etc.

GIRL: (Spoken)
(Sung)
Dined with Jean, Le Pa-vil-lon, then flew right on to St. Mark's Pi-az-za.
FELLOW: (Spoken)
Took a group for on-ion soup at dawn to Les Halles, It nev-er
Str. pizz.
42
ELLA: (Spoken)
GIRL: (Spoken)
shuts Like Chock-Full-Of-Nuts! My Chris-tian Di-or I wore, then tore, got
W.W.
mf
Quasi legato
Vla., Cello
Vlns.
ANOTHER GIRL:
fit-ted for a new Bal-an-cia-ga. Then to Jaques Fath for just one hat---
etc.
3rd GIRL:
got some-thing that will drive you ga-ga. Val-en-ti-na's where I've been; I
Fl.
Str., Picc.

5062

4th GIRL:
ELLA:
ELLA continues.
I do all my shopping etc.
just a-dore Val_ Things with good lines Like things from Kleins!
At Cue: ELLA: Mary Schwartz and Ethel Hotchkiss!
Fast
51
CHORUS: (Sung)
ELLA:
Er-rol Flynn!_ Rin Rin Tin!_
mf Rim Trb. Bss'n.
Tutti
CHORUS:
ELLA:
Ed-mund Gwenn!_ Ren Ren Ten!_
59
CHORUS:
ELLA:
Al-i Kahn!_ Rahn Tan Tan!_
CHORUS: (Spoken)
ELLA:
Ray-mond Mas-sey! Las-sie!
W.W.
p

67
ALL:
That's the way you play the game. Drop that
W.W.
Str., Hrns.
f Tutti
[In 4]
name! Ha-ha!
f
77 (Play off)
f W.W., Str.
3
Fade and stop as JEFF says: Mel!
W.W.

No. 18

The Party's Over

Cue: JEFF: I'll say goodnight to Larry.
(He exits)

20
how you pre-tend, you knew it would end this way. It's time to wind up
Celeste
Cello
Bass
the mas-quer-ade. Just make your mind up the pi-per
28
must be paid. The par-ty's o-ver, The can-dles flick-er and dim.
Celeste
poco rit.
a tempo
p
You danced and dreamed through the night; It seemed to be right, just be-ing with him.
cresc.

36
Now you must wake up; All dreams must end.
mf
Bass
Take off your make - up. The par - ty's o - ver;
pp subito
Celeste
3
46
It's all o - ver, my friend.
W.W., Vlns. 8va
p
Da da da da da da
Da da da da da
You danced and
Fl.
Harp
Celeste
GROUP: (Girls & Boys)
dreamed through the night; It seemed to be right, just be-ing with him. Now you must
+W.W.
Hrn.

No. 18 A Change Of Scene

Salzburg

Cue: SANDOR: I love you.

SUE:
SANDOR:
we, oh so hap-py will be. Oh, where, oh where is this place of mys-ter-y? Where?
p Brass (muted)
Gong
Bright Waltz (In 1)
SANDOR:
24
In Salz - burg by the
+W.W.
f
Str.
mf
sea, Where love and laugh-ter live e-ter-nal-ly. In
Cl., Fl. 8va
32
Salz - burg by the hill, Where gon-do-las go glid-ing by the
SUE:
40
SANDOR:
SUE:
mill. What a thrill, dar-ling! Trop-i-cal nights. Fes-ti-val lights.
colla voce

SANDOR:
SUE: Arriba!
48
Stru-del for two at the mid-night bull fights. In Salz - burg, — love - ly
Fl.
rit.
Hp.gliss.
a tempo
Salz - burg, — Where the fly - ing fish - es play. — Where the
Fl.
W.W.
56
schnit-zel is high as an el - e - phant's eye And the skies are not
pizz. Str., W.W.
Bssn.
64
cloud - y all day. — Come to Salz - burg with me — Lieb-chen!
BOTH:
by the sea! — O - le!
Hp. gliss

72
SANDOR: Come on, Sue. SUE: Oh, Sandor, tell me more! SANDOR: You want more?
(At cue: He looks at his watch.)
(Sung)
In
mf
Br.
Str., W.W.
80
SUE: You said it!
Salz - burg — by the sea, Where all the world's in love with gay Pa -
mf
SUE: You said you love me!
88
SUE: He loves me!
ree. In Salz - burg — on the shore, Where
SUE: (Spoken) San - dor!
(Spoken)
96
SUE:
Gei - sha girls keep com - ing back for more. Lieb - chen! We'll live in
Vln.
Str.
SANDOR:
BOTH:
style, Gold by the pile. Gou - lash for two as we
rit.

104
barge down the Nile. In Salz - burg, love - ly Salz - burg,
Hp. gliss
a tempo
SANDOR:
Where the corn and 'ta - ters grow.
SUE:
In our
Harp
Vlns.
p
112
sweet home sweet home all the roads lead to Rome,
BOTH:
So, my dar - ling, let's
hur - ry and go!
SANDOR: 121
Come to Salz - burg with me - - -
(Spoken)
Lieb - chen!
f
BOTH: (Sung)
By the sea.
O - le!
(Blackout)
attacca

No. 19A Night Club Incidental

and says: It's a ring of counterfeiters, Come on! *Then proceed directly to # 19B fanfare.*

No. 19B Fanfare

Moderately

MASTER OF CEREMONIES: And now, folks, the Pyramid Club presents it's new all-summer revue, featuring music and lyrics by Joe Kitchell!

No. 20 The Midas Touch

Then your kiss is no-va-caine. But I'm al-ways sen-si-tive to
21
[In four]
MALE SINGER: (A la Johnny Ray)
you. You don't see an-y-thing But it
Tutti
Saxs.
p
hurts!
Vlns.
Tho you can't see the pain
Oh, oh how it hurts!
FOUR DANCING BOYS:
The
30 Bright Tempo
Mi-das touch, The might-y, might-y, might-y, might-y
Ten. Sax.
Bass pizz.

Mi-das touch. The Mi - das touch, The
mighty - y, might - y, might - y, might - y Mi-das touch. The Mi - das
touch, The might - y, might - y, Mi-das touch!
Cl.
Ten. Sax.
Trb. 8va bassa
42
Gold — in the morn-ing. Gold — in the eve - ning.
Br.
Piano, Guitar
Ten. Sax.
Br.
Piano, Guitar
Ten. Sax.

Gold— in the sum-mer. Gold— in the win-ter.
50
DANCING GIRLS: (Shouted)
Doc-tor Mi-das said to me: "Be sure and take your vi-ta-min
Br.
Saxs.
G - O - L - D" And that's what he said to me, Hey!
58
Br.
ff
Saxs.

66
Br.,Saxs.
Saxs.
Br.,Saxs.
Saxs.
ff
Rock (Twice as slow)
MALE SINGER:
Gold in all its glo - ry, And that's the sto - ry of the Mi - das
touch.
1st Tpt.
KITCHELL: Wonderful, wonderful. I wrote that song. Dialogue continues.

Long Before I Knew You Reprise And Incidental

No. 21

Cue: KITCHELL: Wait! *(He starts to sing "That's funny - that you love me!")* *Police pull all off stage left.* COP *says:* Come on! *(Blackout)*

(con 8va)
Celeste, Harp
f Str. & Cls.
L.H.
Hrn. Solo
rit.
26
JEFF: (Sings)
I pic-tured some-one who'd walk and talk and smile as you do; Who'd
Str.
make me feel as you do right now. All that was
Hrns., Cello
34
long be-fore I held you,
Long be-fore I kissed you,
E.H. 8va
B.Cl.

Long be-fore I touched you and felt this glow.
42
But now you real-ly are here and now at last I know That
Str.
(Spoken)
long be-fore I knew you, I loved you so.
Doctor Kitchell!
p
rall.
50
JEFF enters phone booth and dials.
play 2 times
pizz.Vla,Cello, Cls.
pp
Stop when telephone voice answers:
Dr. Kitchell's Dental Clinic etc.
Cue:
JEFF starts to dial again.
play 2 times
Stop when telephone voice answers:
Blake Barton's residence etc.
JEFF: That's funny etc.
Mom? Mom! MOM!
(Blackout)
Harp gliss.
Tutti
ff
Hp. ad lib. gliss.

No. 22

I'm Going Back

Cue: ELLA: The trouble is, I don't really know myself who I am.

18
They've got a great big switch-board there—
Where it's just "Hel - lo, good - bye!" It
may be dull, But there I can be just me, my - self and I.
26
A lit - tle mod'ling on the side. Yes, that's where I'll
W.W.
Vln.
be At the Bon - jour Tris - tesse
W.W.
B.Cl., Cello

Bras - siere Com-pa - ny. And if
muted Tpt., W.W.
34
an - y - bod - y asks for El - la, Me - la or Mom,
W.W.
Br.
Tell them that I'm go-ing back where I came from, To the B. T. Bras-si - ere
Com - pa - ny.
Cymb.
42
Free
Broad and steady
(Sarah Vaughn style)
Good-bye, ev'-ry-bod - y; Good-bye, Ma-dame Grim-al - di; Good - bye, Jun - ior Mal - let,
Hp.
gliss.
Str.

San - ta Claus is hit - tin' the road.
Tpt.
Lis-ten to your ma-ma, ma-ma, ma-ma. Eat your spin-ach, ba-by, Eat your spin-ach, ba - by, by the
p
Valse Francaise (In three)
(Spoken)
52
load. La Petite Bergère Restaurant....... adieu. Je ne
Vlns.
Cls.
reviendrai Jamais, jamais, jamais. C'est tous fini, Adieu to yieu. So,
Fl.
Harp
3
60 Allegro
(Sung)
Good - bye, Max, To your dogs and your cats, To the Duke of
W.W.
p

68
Wind-sor and his Duch-ess. Good - bye, Bar - ton,
add Br., pizz. Str.
Kit-chell and Has-tings. At last you're out of my clutch-es. I'll
76
Slow
miss you, but you'll car - ry on. You'll nev - er know that I'm
Str., W.W.
f-p
Str.
Hrns.
f-p
81
In tempo (with great energy, like a jazzy strut)
gone. I'm go-ing back where I can be
Br.
mp
Str.

me, To the Bon - jour Tris - tesse Bras - siere Com-pa - ny.
Br.
And
W.W.
Vlns.
etc.
91
while I'm sit - tin' there I hope that I'll find out
W.W. (8va bassa)
mf Str.
Just what El - la Pe-ter-son is all a - bout, In that Shang - ri - la of
etc.
(loco)

Slow
Molto
lac - y lin-ger - ie, A lit-tle mod-ling on the side, At the
mf Tutti
marcato
Bon - jour Tris-tesse Bras-siere Com - pa - ny.
(Shouted-like Jolson, or Harry Richman) (Sung)
103
Send me my mail there, To the Bon - jour Tris - tesse Com - pa - ny.
f
ff

No. 23 Finale

Cue: HASTINGS: Where is that wonder girl?

No. 24 Curtain Music

17
lot to re-com-mend her for a girl. A fab-u-lous crea-ture with-
out an-y doubt. This is what I'm get-ting so ex-cit-ed a-bout.
25
ALL:
3
Yet when she looks up at me. What does she see?
Saxs., Str.
Tutti
33
Br.
The most en-chant-ing face. His
Saxs. sust.
Tpts.
heart keeps beat-ing fast-er and fast-er and fast-er and now, We're in
divisi
Tutti
Br.
cresc.

43
He met a girl, a won-der-ful girl, A fab - u - lous
Love with a girl, Pla-za O, doub-le four, doub-le
f
girl.
51
three. It's a per-fect re - la - tion-ship, They're
mf
Pla - za O doub - le four, doub-le three.
61 Broadly
And the bells are ring-ing, Ring-ing.
Telephone
8va bassa
attacca

No. 25 Exit Music

37
unis. Tpts.
f

Trbs.
Trb. Solo
W.W.
W.W.
3
Trbs.
Hp. gliss.

unis. Tpts.
sempre f
mf
Moderately (In four)

muted Tpt. Solo
Tutti
cresc.&rit.
a tempo
rall.
sf